CW01095202

ARE YOU SURE OF HEAVEN?

and if so,

ARE YOU LIVING TO THE GLORY OF GOD?

Essential Truths from the Word of God

Published by
Maurice Wylie Media
Your Inspirational Christian Publisher

Publishers' statement: Throughout this book, the love for our God is such that whenever we refer to Him, we honour with capital letters. On the other hand, when referring to the devil, we refuse to acknowledge him with any honour to the point of violating grammatical rule and withholding capitalization.

For more information visit

www.MauriceWylieMedia.com

Contents

Part 1

ARE YOU SURE OF HEAVEN?

Mankind lives in a fallen, difficult, and at times dangerous world. Many find it difficult to know what to believe or how to act in each given situation.

There are so many voices out there, some good and some not so good; some telling the truth, some telling us lies. It is, therefore, necessary that we as citizens of this world are able to tell the difference between truth and lies, between what is right and what is wrong, between what is good and what is evil.

If then we want to know "what is the truth," we need to listen to the One who said: *"I* *am the way, **the Truth** and the life…"* (John 14:6). This is the voice of our Creator, our sustainer, and the voice of the One who is willing to be our Saviour, our guide and helper through life. This is the One who alone can prepare us for this life and for the life hereafter when this earthly journey is over, taking us to be with Himself for eternity. *"For of him, and through him, and to him, are all things: to whom be glory for ever"* Romans 11:36.

Where then can we find these words of truth? They have been inspired, compiled, preserved and handed down to us in a book called the Bible, also called the Word of God. There are 66 separate books contained within the Bible, beginning at Genesis and ending with Revelation. They point us right back to the beginnings of time, and through the prophets, point us forward to the endings of time.

We also have, throughout this precious book, a record of many who lived before us. About how some succeeded in life and about how others failed. About how some believed in God's Word of truth and acted upon it, and about how others believed not, going their own way, leading to a lost life and, tragically, to a lost soul.

Most people cannot read the Word of God in its original language since it was written mainly in Hebrew and Greek. We therefore have to depend upon a translation. As there are many translations of the Bible, it is necessary to find a correct one. There are mainly two types: one that gives a word for word translation, staying as close as possible to the original text, such as we have in the Authorised or the King James Version. The other is where the translators give what they think is the meaning of the text, which is more like a commentary, and therefore unreliable.

Having then found a good word for word translation of the Bible, in order to understand its teachings, its truths, and its doctrines, it is essential to interpret the Bible correctly.

The Bible is a book, although a very sacred one, and should be read as a book; it is God's instruction book to mankind.

It is also good and helpful to understand the reason or the purpose for which the Bible, which is God's Word, has been written.

The Apostle Paul, who was God's penman for much of the New Testament, has given us that reason when writing to his young protégé Timothy.

"And that from a child thou hast known the holy scriptures, which are able to make thee wise unto salvation through faith which is in Christ Jesus. All scripture is given by inspiration of God, and is profitable for doctrine, for reproof, for correction, for instruction in righteousness: that the man of God may be perfect, thoroughly furnished unto all good works" 2 Timothy 3:15-17.

Having then the precious Word of God in our hands, it is essential that we read it for ourselves.

There are those who will say, "The Bible is too difficult to understand. Let us interpret it for you and tell you what you have to do."

No true servant of God will take one away from reading the Scriptures but will rather bring each individual back to God's Word to read it for themselves.

It has rightly been said, "The Bible, God's true revelation to all humanity, is our ultimate authority on all matters about which it speaks. It is not a total mystery, but can be adequately understood by ordinary people in every culture."

We dare not <u>naively</u> trust any other person or denomination with the interpretation of the Scriptures, which affects not only this life but also the life to come.

What then is the best way to approach the Word of God?

The answer is; with a seeking heart.

We are seeking for answers to the perplexities of life.

Answers to the emptiness, the selfishness, and the 'wickedness' of the human heart.[1]

Did God create mankind with a wicked heart? No. *"God saw everything that He has made and behold it was very good"* Genesis 1:31.

How then do we find ourselves living in a sad, sinful world?

Reading through Genesis chapter 3, we find out where and when it all went wrong; how mankind became separated from God his Creator through the disobedience of our first parents, Adam and Eve.

Also, in the same chapter, we begin to see something of the grace of our great God, by a veiled reference as to how mankind could be reunited again with his Maker. First, in chapter 3:15, as to how the seed of

1. Jeremiah 17:9

a woman (with reference to Christ) would bruise the head of the serpent, who brought death and separation. Then in verse 21, the Plan of Redemption was given in type, when another died a substitutionary death in place of Adam and Eve, that they might be clothed in the covering of The One sacrificed.

This was pointing forward to the death and sacrifice of Jesus Christ for man's sins, that all who trust in Him might be clothed with His righteousness.

When the Son of God came down to earth, in God's appointed time, in the person of the Lord Jesus Christ, it was John the Baptist who identified Him saying: *"…Behold the Lamb of God, which taketh away the sin of the world"* John 1:29.

Then in John chapter 3, the Lord Jesus, while speaking with Nicodemus, gave the reason for His coming into the world: *"For God so loved the world, that He gave*

His only begotten Son, that whosoever believeth in Him should not perish, but have everlasting life." (v16)

Salvation then is a gift of God the Father.
Ephesians 2:8-9

Salvation was purchased by God the Son.
1 Timothy 1:15

Salvation is administered by God the Holy Spirit. John 3:6, 8

The first essential "Truth" of Scripture is that: *"All have sinned, and come short of the glory of God"* Romans 3:23.

The second alarming "Truth" of Scripture is that: *"The wages of sin is death"* Romans 6:23.

As God said to Adam: *"For in the day that thou eatest thereof thou shalt surely die"* Genesis 2:17.

"Wherefore, as by one man sin entered into the world, and death by sin; and so death

passed upon all men, for that all have sinned" Romans 5:12.

The third great "Truth" of Scripture is that: *"Christ Jesus came into the world to save sinners"* 1 Timothy 1:15.

"For God so loved the world, that he gave his only begotten Son, that whosoever believeth in him should not perish, but have everlasting life" John 3:16.

What then is God asking us to believe concerning His Son?

God through His Word is asking us to believe:

That Jesus Christ was and is God.[2]

That Jesus Christ being God took upon Himself the form and likeness of man. The God man.[3]

---

2. Philippians 2:6
3. Philippians 2:7

That Jesus Christ, being now perfect God and perfect man, was able and so wonderfully willing to be man's sinless substitute, becoming obedient unto death, even the death of the cross.[4]

That Jesus Christ was raised from the dead to be seated at the right hand of God the Father; both a Prince and a Saviour.[5]

Both Scripture and world history will tell us this event took place 2000 years ago at a city called Jerusalem, and is detailed for us in the New Testament Gospels.

What then must I do to be saved?

This question was asked of the Apostle Paul in Acts 16:30.

The answer was: *"Believe on the Lord Jesus Christ, and thou shalt be saved"* Acts 16:31.

One of the shortest prayers for salvation in

4. Philippians 2:8
5. Philippians 2:9-11, Acts 5:31

the Bible is recorded for us in Luke 18:13: *"God be merciful to me a sinner."*

Can we not detect faith together with both humility and sincerity in this short prayer?

In the very next verse, this prayer was given as an example of how to call upon the name of the Lord for salvation, by none other than our Saviour Himself, even the Lord Jesus Christ. (Luke 18:14)

In this same passage, we have been given an example of how not to pray.[6]

Although salvation is an act of God, which happens in a moment, there is a process leading up to that moment, and continuing on from it, given by the Apostle Paul in Ephesians 1:13-14:

"In whom ye also trusted, after that ye heard the word of truth, the gospel of your salvation: in whom also after that ye believed, ye were sealed with that holy

---

6. Luke 18:9-14

Spirit of promise, which is the earnest of our inheritance until the redemption of the purchased possession, unto the praise of his glory."

Notice in this verse of Scripture how that the people heard, they believed, and they were sealed.

They **heard** God's Word of Truth.

They **believed** the Gospel. (*"…How that Christ died for our sins according to the Scriptures; and that He was buried and that He rose again the third day according to the Scriptures")* 1 Corinthians 15:3-4.

They were **sealed** with the Holy Spirit of promise.

Each believer is indwelled by God's Holy Spirit from when they believed until they leave this world to be with Christ for ever, as the earnest, or as a foretaste of their inheritance in Christ.[7]

7. Ephesians 1:13-14

Not only is each believer indwelled by the Holy Spirit from the moment of salvation, but as the same chapter emphasises, speaking of each believer as being in Christ. Ephesians 1:7 reads: *"In whom we have redemption through His blood, the forgiveness of sins, according to the riches of His grace."*

Whenever a person believes the Gospel from the heart and trusts in the Lord Jesus Christ for salvation, that believer is placed into the spiritual body of Jesus Christ[8] and into the merits of His Redeeming work.[9]

What then are the results of this great redeeming and transforming work of God in the life of the believer?

To answer that question, we turn to 2 Corinthians 5:17: *"Therefore if any man be in Christ, he is a new creature: **old things** are passed away; behold, **all things are become new.**"*

---

8. 1 Corinthians 12:13
9. Romans 6:3

To understand something of the old things the believer has been delivered from, and about the new life they have been brought into by the riches of God's mercy and the abundance of God's grace, (read from Ephesians 2:1-10).

What should the believer's response be to what God has delivered us from and to what God has brought us into?

The Apostle Paul sets this out in Romans 12.

v1 *"I beseech you therefore, brethren, by the mercies of God, that ye present your bodies a living sacrifice, holy, acceptable unto God, which is your reasonable service."*

v2 *"And be not conformed to this world: but be ye transformed by the renewing of your mind, that ye may prove what is that good, and acceptable, and perfect, will of God."*

This is the only way to live a successful Christian life to the glory of God.

As the Lord Jesus said; *"If any man will come after me, let him deny himself, and take up his cross, and follow me"* Matthew 16:24.

What the Lord is asking His people to deny is the old sinful nature with which we were born, and indeed is still with us after coming to Him.[10]

That is:
the sinful desires of the old nature.
the sinful desires of the world.
the sinful desires of the devil.

Why the Lord Jesus is asking the believer to take up his cross is because this denying of self is not just a once for all experience, as salvation, but a daily exercise; as the Apostle Paul himself said: *"I die daily"* (1 Corinthians 9:27, 15:31). Only then can a follower of Jesus Christ experience fully the unhindered workings of the Holy Spirit; only then will the fruit of the Spirit become a reality; only then can we be led in the paths of righteousness for His name's sake.

---

10. Romans 7:15-25

Paul said; *"I am crucified with Christ: nevertheless I live; yet not I, but Christ liveth in me: and the life which I now live in the flesh I live by the faith of the Son of God, who loved me, and gave himself for me"* Galatians 2:20.

It is in these words that we find the secret of Paul's successful Christian living.

It was a life of faith.

It was standing down and allowing the Spirit of God and of the Lord Jesus Christ to take over.

If any believer could have confidence in their own abilities, it would have been Paul.

They are listed in Philippians 3:4-6.

In verses 7-14 of this same chapter we have been given a glimpse into how Paul lived.

He is dying to the old Paul that the new

Paul might be resurrected in the power and in the righteousness of God, which is by faith.

This is what the Apostle Paul called his *"reasonable service"* (Romans 12:1). This is what Paul called his *"high calling"* (Philippians 3:14).

Part 2

ARE YOU THEN LIVING TO THE GLORY OF GOD?

Obviously, not all Christians are as faithful or as dedicated as the Apostle Paul was.

Not only is this so today, but even back in biblical times, there were those who were not living to the glory of God. But why?

The simple answer is that the Christian life is a battle. That is why the Apostle said, *"I have fought the good fight."* He also described the believer as a soldier of Jesus Christ.[11]

And as a soldier, it is advisable to put on the whole amour of God (Ephesians 6:10-11)

11. 2 Timothy 2:3

because the enemy is subtle and the glory of God and our Saviour Jesus Christ is at stake.

Who then is this enemy? It is the same enemy of God and God's people that we find throughout the Bible. We hear him whispering to Eve, *"Thou shalt not surely die."* Yes, we find him stalking God's people and seeking to thwart God's purposes throughout Scripture. He is given his full name in Revelation 12:9 and 20:2, *"The great dragon was cast out, that old serpent, called the devil, and satan, which deceiveth the whole world."*

The Lord Jesus gave him his full pedigree when speaking with those who would eventually deliver Him to be crucified: *"Ye are of your father the devil, and the lusts of your father ye will do. He was a murderer from the beginning, and abode not in the truth, because there is no truth in him. When he speaketh a lie, he speaketh of his own: for he is a liar, and the father of it"* John 8:44. What an enemy!

Want to see him in action against a man of God?
Read the life of Job.

Our consolation is that he is under the complete control of God.

"And the LORD said unto satan, Behold, all that he hath is in thy power; only upon himself put not forth thine hand. So satan went forth from the presence of the LORD" Job 1:12.

Note: Job's wife was part of Job; everything else, satan destroyed.

And again, when satan sought to destroy Job's body, God said: *"And the LORD said unto satan, Behold, he is in thine hand; but save his life"* Job 2:6. The life of a believer is monitored by the Lord, every thought, word and deed. (Read Psalm 139)

And will not allow us to be tempted more

than we are able to bear 1 Corinthians 10:13. Does God cause us to be tempted? No.

But He allows us to be tempted to prove us.

It was the Spirit of God who led our Saviour into the wilderness to be tempted. But it was the devil who did the tempting.[12]

God allowed it to prove the sinlessness of His Son.

In Job's case, it was the devil who moved God to allow Job's severe testing.[13]

God allowed it because He acknowledged Job's strong faith and faithfulness. Whenever God allows His children to be tempted, He will, with the temptation, make a way of escape.[14]

In the face of temptation, it will be helpful if we keep in mind that this life is for us all, a preparation for eternity: where we are to

---

12. Matthew 4:1
13. Job 2:5
14. 1 Corinthians 10:13

spend it, in heaven or hell, and what place or position we will have in either place?

The battle or the dispute is ultimately between the Lord God of heaven, and satan, the would-be God, who is against everything God stands for.

While following the God of heaven, He may lead us through deep waters to prove us, but it will be on a road that will lead to glory.

For anyone to follow and give themselves to the god of this world, who is satan, he can drag them down to the lowest hell.[15]

These are alarming facts; these are Biblical truths to which we should give heed.

It is lovely to see someone young, or even not so young, bow in repentance towards God, and have faith in our Lord Jesus Christ (Acts 20:21), acknowledging that: *"All have sinned, and come short of the glory*

---

15. Psalm 86.13

of God." Romans 3:23, Psalm 51:5, accepting: "That *Christ died for our sins according to the Scriptures"* 1 Corinthians 15:3, Romans 4:25.

Then, going on to speak of their faith and trust in the Lord Jesus Christ.[16]

Scripture teaches us that satan cannot hinder the Holy Spirit of God from opening the minds and the understanding of a person to the truth of the Gospel, or His leading them to the place of salvation. But he will seek to hinder that person from growing in grace, and to hinder that new believer's walk with God; seeking, if possible, to knock them out of the race and nullify their usefulness for God; although he can never take away the salvation of a child of God.[17]

To answer the question: Why are there so many half-hearted Christians in the world today?

Scripture has set out for us the first steps of a new, born-again believer in Christ. They

16. Romans 10:9, 1:16
17. John 10:27-29, Romans 8:35-39

are somewhat similar to that of a natural
new-born babe.

The first thing a new, spiritual born babe will
be expected to do is to cry; in other words, to
pray, calling upon the name of the Lord for
mercy and salvation. (The first sign the Lord
gave that Saul's conversion was genuine, was:
"Behold he prayeth" (Acts 9:11).

Again, this should be followed by a desire
in the new believer for *"the sincere* (or pure)
milk of the Word (of God) *that ye may grow
thereby."* 1 Peter 2:2. Then, like a natural baby,
the new born-again believer in Christ will
need to be washed by reading the Word
of God, understand things which might
displease the Lord, and be guided in a better
way; being enabled to do so by the Holy
Spirit abiding within the heart and the life
of every believer. (John 15:3, 17:17).

As the spiritual babe in Christ begins
to grow or should begin to mature, that
relationship with their Saviour and their

God, is somewhat similar to that between a young man and his wife.[18]

For that earthly bond and relationship to grow and prosper, there needs to be a love for each other, together with a fear of losing the others' bond of communion and fellowship; then sandwiched between love and fear, there needs to be the qualities of respect and faithfulness.

Coming back to the question – Why are so many Christians not living to their full potential, not living to the glory of God their Saviour?

Christians who live defeated lives: failing to overcome in the hour of temptation, failing to obey the Word of God, and having lost communion with God the Holy Spirit who dwells within the heart of every believer.

One of the underlying reasons for such half-hearted Christianity is a half-hearted

18. Ephesians 5:28-32

sense of repentance toward God[19]. A failure to understand how lost, hopeless and sinful we were in the eyes of God before being sought and found by Him, our Creator and our Saviour[20]. A failure to appreciate the cost of our redemption. How the Lord of glory took on Himself the form of man and being found in fashion a man, He humbled Himself and became obedient unto death, even the death of the cross[21].

A failure to remember that our lovely Saviour, who, although being despised and rejected by the world, yet set His face to go all the way to Jerusalem, that He might, through death, redeem a people for His name. A failure to understand that every sin has to be accounted for, every sin had to be atoned for, including the sins of those who are now the children of God – past, present and future (1 John 2:1-2).

The sad fact is that many professing Christians are lost in a fog of acceptable

19. Acts 20:21
20. Jeremiah 17:9
21. Philippians 2:5-11

Christianity, but not really going anywhere in God. The mediocre Christian who is not really going forward with God, will want to hold onto as much of this world as possible while at the same time doing the things Christians do.

If, on the other hand, we mean business with God and want to be led forward in the ways of God. We need to start by getting down to God's instruction book, to God's road-map of life (The Word of God).

The first thing we should learn is that no man can serve two masters. We cannot love the ways of the world and love the Lord at the same time.

The starting point is that: "Ye are not on your own. *For ye are bought with a price: therefore glorify God in your body, and in your spirit, which are God's*" 1 Corinthians 6:19-20. And what a price was paid by our Saviour.

This leads us to two very important verses in Romans 12:1-2.

"I beseech you therefore, brethren, by the mercies of God, that ye present your bodies a living sacrifice, holy, acceptable unto God, which is your reasonable service. And be not conformed to this world: but be ye transformed by the renewing of your mind, that ye may prove what is that good, and acceptable, and perfect, will of God."

Who did we belong to before we were bought, sought and found by God? The answer is, satan. Is it not reasonable that we should place our lives and our bodies into the hands and into the will of Him who purchased us? In these two verses, we find the key to a fulfilled Christian life.

There is an idea that if I give my life completely into the hands of God, I will not be able to do the things that I would like to do; I will miss all the fun! But hold on, where did that idea come from?

The only things the Lord will want to take from you are the things that are spoiling your life, which could be summed up in two words, namely, sin and selfishness.

That stands in sharp contrast to what the Lord wants to give us, which is: Love, joy, peace, longsuffering, gentleness, goodness, faith, meekness, temperance [22]. Together with a strong faith and a clear conscience. What a character that list will turn any believer into. [23]

What a way to lay one's head on the pillow each night and to rise the following morning to go forward in the will of God and to the glory of God.

But we need to remember that we live in a world where a great battle is taking place between the Lord God of heaven, and the would-be God, who is satan.

This battle is being carried on in the minds, hearts and lives of earth's citizens - between

22. Galatians 5:22-23
23. 1 Timothy 1:19

those who are for God, and those who are against God. Between those who are active to various degrees on both sides, together with many who are inactive in this battle.

But it must be said that those who are not for God, those who have not been born-again into the family of God, are still under the power of darkness, still travelling on that road unto which we were born, a road that will eventually lead to destruction.[24]

The origins of this war on earth go back to the fall, which we read about in Genesis chapter 3. That is when sin and ungodliness entered into God's creation; the effects of which are still to be seen all around us to this day. We see it in the vegetable world when those who grow our food have to battle against the thorn and the thistle. We see it in the animal world when they often reach the point of devouring one another. In fact, for some of them, it is a way of life. But for now, we are concerned about the human world.

---

24. John 3:36

How then did the fall affect the human race?

First of all, mankind is not part of the animal kingdom, as some would have us think. God made man in His own image, with that extra dimension called – spirit; which is that capacity for God, that need of God, that ability to commune with God. Yes, we have been made by God and for God; body, soul and spirit.[25]

Maybe we should ask the evolutionists have they ever seen a monkey praying to God?

It was during the fall of Genesis chapter 3 that mankind became separated from God his Creator, only to fall under the dominion of satan.

But God has so graciously and so wonderfully set in motion His eternal plan whereby mankind could be brought back to Himself to live for His glory. This is the good news of the Bible, the Word of God,

25. Genesis 1:27, Proverbs 20:27, Romans 8:16

described in the New Testament as the Gospel.

Herein lies the source of this battle that is being carried on in this world today. It began in heaven when satan, who was a beautiful created angel of God, began to be lifted up with pride, and said: *"I will be like the Most High, I will exalt my throne above the stars of God"* Isaiah 14:13-14. The Lord Jesus was later to say: *"I beheld satan as lightning fall from heaven"* Luke 10:18.

When he landed on earth, he must have been very angry, and still is to this day.

In Genesis chapter 3, we find him in the garden of Eden commencing his work of deception, lies and violence against everything and everyone who belongs to God.

We as human beings should ever be mindful that the devil is a powerful being, and it is only by the power and by the grace of God so freely offered in the Gospel that we can ever be delivered from his evil grasp and given the ability to live free from his soul-destroying abilities. Even Michael the archangel addressed him with consideration saying: *"The Lord rebuke thee"* (Jude verse 9).

He is regarded in Scripture as a prince, even though a prince of darkness. But thankfully, he, the prince of this evil world, is judged,[26] and awaiting his incarceration into that place prepared for him.[27]

As we have said before, the devil cannot prevent the triune God from drawing men and women out of the power of darkness into the kingdom of His own dear Son, but the devil and his demons will ever seek to make life difficult for them.

The problem for the believer is that the old fallen nature, called in Scripture 'the old man' (Ephesians 4:22), which the believer will have,

---

26. John 16:11
27. Matthew 25:41

or should have died to, is still with us, seeking to get back into control, seeking to be revived, seeking for nourishment, seeking to be fed.

The Apostle Paul wrote about this problem in his early Christian life. Read through Romans chapter 6 and 7, where he eventually says: *"O wretched man that I am! who shall deliver me from the body of this death? I thank God through Jesus Christ our Lord. So then with the mind I myself serve the law of God; but with the flesh the law of sin"* Romans 7:24-25. Going on to say in Romans 8:2: *"For the law of the Spirit of life in Christ Jesus hath made me free from the law of sin and death."*

This is where the Apostle Paul found the place of victory: *"For the law of the Spirit of life in Christ Jesus hath made me free from the law of sin and death."*

The old Paul has been laid to rest. This is when he could say, as we quoted; *"I am crucified with Christ: nevertheless I live; yet not I, but Christ liveth in me: and the life which I now live in the flesh I live by the faith of the Son of God, who loved me, and gave himself for me"* Galatians 2:20. From then on, Paul went on to live a life to the glory of God. A life that the world is still benefiting from to this day, through his writings of God's Word.

Did the Apostle Paul lose out then by his total commitment to God? No!

It was the Lord Jesus who said, *"Except a corn of wheat fall into the ground and die, it abideth alone: but if it die, it bringeth forth much fruit. He that loveth his life shall lose it; and he that hateth his life in this world shall keep it unto life eternal"* John 12:24-25.

It must be noted that even though the Apostle had made a total commitment to God and had made a total break with this present evil world, we gather that he had to keep an eye on that old Paul; that old nature, when he said… *"But I keep under my body, and bring it into subjection: lest that by any means, when I have preached to others, I myself should be a castaway"* 1 Corinthians 9:27. This could be followed by his advice to the believers at Rome: *"But put ye on the Lord Jesus Christ, and make not <u>provision</u> for the flesh, to fulfil the lusts thereof"* Romans 13:14.

It is that word **provision**, that we need to be careful with. Victory can be ours if we want it; it is only a sincere prayer away.

But if we start catering for the old sinful nature, desires may well be aroused that become strong in the hour of temptation. So strong that we might not even want to pray for victory in the Lord Jesus Christ.

What we have been considering here has to do very much with personal Christianity, which is very important, and an area that must be kept under constant review. That continual relationship between the believer and his God, his Saviour and his Lord.

THY NEIGHBOUR

In Matthew, one of the religious leaders of his day asked the Lord Jesus Christ about the law and the commandments of the Scriptures.

The answer that he received was, *"Thou shalt love the Lord thy God with all thy heart, and with all thy soul, and with all thy mind. This is the first and great commandment. And the second is like unto it, Thou shalt love thy neighbour as thyself. On these two commandments hang all the law and the prophets"* Matthew 22:37-40. Yes, "Thy neighbour!" That is where the fun starts, and sometimes, not so much fun.

Thy neighbour in the home, thy neighbour at school, thy neighbour in the workplace, thy neighbour in a church or religious setting, thy neighbour out in the world at large.

Some of our neighbours will be our friends, some will be indifferent towards us, others will want to oppose us, still, others will be against anything and everything to do with Christianity.

The Lord Jesus gave the people of His day some good advice on how to live with our neighbour: "*Therefore all things whatsoever ye would that men should do to you, do ye even so to them: for this is the law and the prophets*" Matthew 7:12.

In this battle of life, what are the weapons of this present evil world against the people and the work of the Lord? They will despise and reject: that is the reproach of men; they will verbally abuse; they will falsely accuse; they will harass and persecute, seeking to take away our freedom and eventually, in some cases, to take our life.

How then should the child of God respond to such treatment? First of all, the believers battle is not so much against our poor, blind, devil inspired neighbour as against the powers of darkness.[28]

---

28. Ephesians 6:12

Secondly, even our devilish neighbour is under God's restraining power. He will not allow us to be tempted more than we are able to bear.[29]

Thirdly, the child of God should be careful not to invite trouble by behaving in an unacceptable way.

In this battle of life, both sides need weapons. We have been considering what the weapons of this evil world are. What then are the God-given weapons of the man, woman or young person of God?

We are referring again to the Apostle Paul, who said: *"for the weapons of our warfare are not carnal, but mighty through God"* 2 Corinthians 10:4. The believer's enemy is a spiritual enemy[30]. So, the believer's weapons are spiritual; they are mighty through God.

What then about the antics of our devil-inspired neighbour? Should the evildoer

29. 1 Corinthians 10:13
30. Ephesians 6

not then be brought to book and punished for their evil deeds?

Yes, but not by the individual believer. That is the responsibility of the powers that be, as we read in Romans 13:1: *"Let every soul be subject unto the higher powers. For there is no power but of God: the powers that be are ordained of God."* It is the responsibility of the State, to encourage that which is good, and take action against that which is evil.[31]

If a government fails to do so, then that country is in trouble. For, *"Righteousness exalteth a nation: but sin is a reproach to any people"* Proverbs 14:34.

As this then is a spiritual battle for the individual believer, our first approach should be to exercise those spiritual graces which are the fruit of the Spirit.

Again, these are listed in Galatians chapter 5:22-23.

---

31. Romans 13:4

The first of these are for the support and enjoyment of the believer: Love, Joy and Peace. The second three are to be exercised towards our neighbour: Longsuffering, Gentleness, Goodness.

Will the man of the world not then take advantage of someone who behaves in such a gentle way?

Yes, perhaps, but we must understand that in this battle of life, we are not on our own. There is the enemy, there is you, and most importantly, there is the Lord, who has promised never to leave us or forsake us. He is saying: *"My grace is sufficient for thee."* Grace to endure hardness as a good soldier, grace to fight, having put on the whole armour of God.

As for the enemy, he will have to get past the Lord before he can touch you, and sometimes the Lord will allow him past to test you, and to strengthen you.[32]

---

32. 1 Corinthians 10:13

We should also remember that we, as believers, are in Christ. Every wrong and every hurt we have to endure is felt by the Lord, who has announced a great condemnation against those who behave in such a way: *"It is impossible but that offences will come: but woe unto him, through whom they come! It were better for him that a millstone were hanged about his neck, and he cast into the sea, than that he should offend one of these little ones"* Luke 17:1-2. When offended, it is natural for the child of God to hit back in the same way, using the same worldly weapons. At a time like this, we need to remind ourselves again that the weapons of our warfare are not carnal but spiritual.

To find out how believers should prepare themselves for the battle of life, let us turn to Paul's letter to the church at Ephesus: *"Finally, my brethren, be strong in the Lord, and in the power of his might. Put on the whole armour of God, that ye may be able to stand against the wiles of the devil. For we wrestle not against flesh and blood, but against principalities, against powers, against the rulers of the darkness of this world, against spiritual wickedness in high places. Wherefore take unto you the whole armour of God, that ye may be able to withstand in the evil day, and having done all, to stand"* Ephesians 6:10-13. The first thing we learn from these verses is that the child of God is not fighting the battle of life from the standpoint of weakness, but rather in the power of God, as we rest in Him: *"… if God be for us, who can be against us?"* Romans 8:31.

Then we are reminded about the wiles - the sly trickery of the devil: and about the fact that the battle is not against our neighbour, but against the powers of darkness. Therefore, the advice is not only given once but twice – to put on the whole armour of God.

As we read on into verses 14 and 15, we will notice that the emphasis is not about hurting or defeating the enemy - that is

God's part - but rather about keeping the enemy from defeating us and hindering us from doing the will of God, and from enjoying fellowship with God.

Is this not the position where we find so many of God's people today? With lives that are not being lived to the glory of God.

So, the message given in these verses is about how to stand fast in the Lord, and upon all that He has done for us. It is about how we can continue moving forward with God.

And to enable us to do that, the writer begins by focusing on three main areas of the believer's life, which are; the head, the heart and the feet.

Verses 14-15 reads: *"Stand therefore, having your **loins** girt about with truth, and having on the breastplate of righteousness. and your feet shod with the preparation of the gospel of peace."*

The term **'loins'** mentioned here is referring to the loins of the mind. This is confirmed by what we read in 1 Peter 1:13: *"Wherefore gird up the loins of your mind."*

The mind is a wonderful part of the human being. It is where we receive knowledge and instruction to live by. So it is vital that the source of our information is true.

There are many voices out there, but in all the world, there is only one source of absolute truth. It is the Lord Jesus Christ who said: *"I am the way, the truth, and the life: no man cometh unto the Father, but by me"* John 14:6. Again, when our Saviour was praying to God the Father for those who would be His followers, He said: *"Sanctify them through thy truth: thy word is truth"* John 17:17.

In Psalm 12:6, we read: *"The words of the LORD are pure words: as silver tried in a furnace of earth, purified seven times."*

Psalm 119 has many things to say about the Word of God, including the truth of God's

Word: *"Thy Word is true from the beginning; and every one of Thy righteous judgements endureth for ever"* Psalm 119:160. So it is from God's Word that our minds can have understanding concerning the ways of God, the will of God, and the purposes of God for which we were created.

But it is with our hearts that we act upon that information; that is where the decisions are made. The heart is that place that lies at the very centre of one's being.

In Proverbs 4:23, we read: *"Keep thy heart with all diligence; for out of it are the issues of life."*

It is the place where the unregenerate will first hear the call of God; through creation (Romans 1), through conscience (Romans 2:15), and through God's Word.

Again, we refer to Ephesians 1:13, which sets out the steps by which we are saved by grace through the Word of God.

"In whom ye also trusted, after that ye heard the word of truth, the gospel of your salvation: in whom also after that ye believed, ye were sealed with that holy Spirit of promise" Ephesians 1:13. *"For with the heart man believeth unto righteousness; and with the mouth confession is made unto salvation"* Romans 10:10. We see, then, that the heart is such an important part of the believers' life, the dwelling place of the Holy Spirit and the administration centre of one's being. We can be sure that is where the devil will aim for with his fiery darts. We find in James 3:6-8, how the tongue is an unruly evil, and can be set on fire of hell.

Such is the tongue of the wicked, and if allowed to penetrate, could cut a believer's feelings to the very quick.

Protection for the heart is given in Ephesians 6:13-14 as the breastplate of righteousness. This is a righteousness which comes from God through faith. We read in Genesis 15:6 and Romans 4:3, how that Abraham believed God, and it was counted unto him for righteousness.

As has been said, "Each believer has been made the righteousness of God in Christ. The breastplate of righteousness is the working out of what God had wrought within. It is obedience to the Word of God learned in the head; it is a clear conscience."

The second piece of armour used to guard the heart is found in verse 16: *"taking the shield of faith, wherewith ye shall be able to quench all the fiery darts of the wicked."*

Faith in the Word of God and faith in the God of that Word: *"putting on the breastplate of faith and love; and for an helmet, the hope of salvation"* 1 Thessalonians 5:8.

If it is with the head the believer can learn the will of God, and with the heart those instructions are obeyed, it is the 'feet' that carry the believer into action. As we read in Psalm 37:23: *"The steps of a good man are ordered by the Lord, and he delighted in his way;"* the feet being a symbol of our walk with God. It is a walk that could involve different members of our body.

For the Apostle Paul, it meant, together with his intellect, the use of his lips and his hands, both to preach and to write the Word of God.

To Mary was given the great honour of becoming the handmaiden of the Lord.[33]

Yet, for every believer it also means being *"kind one to another, tenderhearted, forgiving one another, even as God for Christ's sake hath forgiven you"* Ephesians 4:32.

Our passage continues with the words: *"And your feet shod with the preparation of the gospel of peace"* Ephesians 6:15.

If throughout Scripture, the purpose of the believer's life is the glory of God, then we can learn from verse 15 that the focus of the believer's life is the Gospel; the good news about God's great provision, through His Son Jesus Christ. How that lost perishing sinners can be forgiven and clothed upon

---

33. Luke 1:38

with the righteousness of God and prepared
to meet their Maker. This is what this world
is all about.

It was while providing this great salvation
that our Saviour's hands, together with His
head, heart and feet, were pierced so that
the believer's walk and the believer's work
might be lived to the honour of His Name,
and dedicated to His Gospel of peace.[34]
"And your feet shod" v15. No soldier would
be found going out to battle tiptoeing about
in bare feet. Neither should the soldier of
Jesus Christ, but should rather be found
standing firm with confidence in God's
great provision through His Son Jesus
Christ, enshrined in the Gospel message.

Not missing the word "preparation," *"shod
with the preparation of the gospel of peace."*

If God has so wonderfully prepared for
us, all that we need in the Gospel, then it
is for the born-again believer to live out
and speak out that same Gospel message.

34. Isaiah 52:7, Romans 10:15

If God's will is learned in the head or the mind and consented to in the heart, then the feet stand prepared to move out to the will of God, not alone, because God has promised never to leave us or forsake us. We can say: *"He leadeth me in the paths of righteousness for His names sake"* Psalm 23:3.Not forgetting the words of the Lord Jesus in Matthew 11:28-30: *"Come unto me, all ye that labour and are heavy laden, and I will give you rest. Take my yoke upon you, and learn of me; for I am meek and lowly in heart: and ye shall find rest unto your souls. For my yoke is easy, and my burden is light."*

What a privilege it is to plough the furrow of life in unison with our Saviour and our God.

We will notice in Ephesians 6:15, that the type of Gospel which God has so graciously given to us, is the Gospel of peace. Although the child of God is called to be a soldier of Jesus Christ, and as the Apostle Paul has said, "to fight the good fight of faith," our warfare is not one of an offensive nature, but rather one of defence, against a devil-inspired neighbour or such, who would seek to destroy our faith, and to hinder our walk with God.

Another occasion where the believer is called upon to stand firm is against so-called Christian leaders and high churchmen; especially when they attempt to undermine the essential doctrines of the Christian faith such as the inspiration of Scripture, the virgin birth of Jesus Christ, the all-sufficiency of His atoning death, and the reality of His resurrection.

Again, at a time like this, we need to remind ourselves that the weapons of our warfare are not carnal (of this world), but spiritual.

This is a time when the believer and the true church leaders need to reach for that part of Christian armour mentioned in verse 17: *"the sword of the Spirit, which is the word of God,"* as a means of challenging those who deny these great truths of Scripture. *"For the word of God is quick, and powerful, and sharper than any twoedged sword, piercing even to the dividing asunder of soul and spirit, and of the joints and marrow, and is a discerner of the thoughts and intents of the heart"* Hebrews 4:12. What a weapon!

The writer in the little epistle of Jude v3 speaks about: *"earnestly contend for the faith which was once delivered unto the saints."* Meaning to stand fast, to reaffirm the essential truths of the Gospel clearly set forth in the Word of God.

The Word of God is a weapon which every believer should learn to use.

The Apostle Paul, in his epistle to Ephesians, has many things to say about the Gospel:

In Ephesians He writes about the
Truth of the Gospel. (1:13)
Promise of the Gospel. (3:6)
Preparation of the Gospel. (6:15)
Mystery of the Gospel. (6:19)
Power of the Gospel. (Romans 1:16)

Although the Gospel is the most dynamic, essential, and life-changing message ever to reach earth from heaven, through Jesus Christ our Saviour, it is still a message of peace, as we read in Ephesians 6:15.

When the Son of God, the Lord Jesus Christ, one of whose titles is 'The Prince of Peace' (Isaiah 9:6), came down to earth to be the Saviour of the world, His birth was announced by the heavenly host of angels saying: *"Glory to God in the highest, and on earth peace, good will toward men"* Luke 2:14. The gospel message, so wonderfully provided by our Saviour, is indeed a message of peace to all who will believe.

To every believer, it first provides peace with God. As our Bible says: *"Therefore being justified by faith, we have <u>peace with God</u> through our Lord Jesus Christ"* Romans 5:1. That is salvation!

The believer can also experience the peace of God. As we read in Philippians 4:6-7: *"Be careful for nothing; but in every thing by* *prayer and supplication with thanksgiving let your requests be made known unto God. And the <u>peace of God</u>, which passeth all understanding, shall keep your hearts and minds through Christ Jesus."* That is fellowship with God.

We also read in John 14:27, words spoken by the Lord Jesus at the end of His earthly ministry: *"Peace I leave with you, my peace I give unto you: not as the world giveth, give I unto you. Let not your heart be troubled, neither let it be afraid."*

The Peace of God is administered by the Holy Spirit who indwells every believer, as we read in Galatians 5:22-23. This can be the portion of every believer who is walking in fellowship with God.

And if possible, this way of peace should be extended toward our neighbour as we read in Romans 12:18: *"If it be possible, as much as lieth in you, live peaceably with all men."*

On the contrary, with the false religions of the world, we will find an element of protective violence.

Their people must be kept away from the truth, and any who would come with the truth must be kept away from their people. What a sad situation!

Part 3

PREPARED FOR HEAVEN?

Again, I would like to ask the question are you prepared for heaven? If not, would you like to be? If so, then that desire of going to heaven can only come from the Lord our God. It is the voice of the Spirit of God, calling you out of darkness. A darkness with which the devil, the god of this world, seeks to keep us captive according to 2 Corinthians 4:4,6: *"In whom the god of this world hath blinded the minds of them which believe not, lest the light of the glorious gospel of Christ, who is the image of God, should shine unto them."*

So, if God has broken through that shroud of darkness, and you are hearing His call, then if you ever want to be in heaven, this is an opportunity not to be missed, because it is the voice of the One who wants you to be there; the voice of the One, who at a tremendous cost, made it possible for you to be there, 1 Peter 2:24. God's salvation is a free gift. It is all of grace, but it is a gift that must be accepted, and it must be accepted in all sincerity, that is, in… *"repentance toward God, and faith toward our Lord Jesus Christ"* Acts 20:21. Repentance in the light of our own lost, fallen, and hopeless situation, and in the light of God's great provision and salvation through Jesus Christ.

We must come like the poor man we read about in Luke 18:13-14, who cried: *"God be merciful to me a sinner. I tell you, this man went down to his house justified."*

Because the Lord Jesus has said: *"All that the Father giveth me shall come to me; and him that cometh to me I will in no wise cast out"* John 6:37.

Have you come?

*"Oh that men would praise the L*ORD *for his goodness, and for his wonderful works to the children of men"* Psalms 107:31.

INSPIRED TO WRITE A BOOK?

Contact
Maurice Wylie Media
Your Inspirational Christian Publisher

Based in Northern Ireland and distributing
around the world.

www.MauriceWylieMedia.com